Moments

Moments

Selected by Lee Bennett Hopkins
Illustrated by Michael Hague

HARCOURT BRACE JOVANOVICH
NEW YORK AND LONDON

TO

Charles John Egita—

FOR MANY REASONS

THROUGH ALL THE SEASONS

Printed in the United States of America

LIBRARY OF CONGRESS CATALOGING IN PUBLICATION DATA

Main entry under title:
Moments.
Includes indexes.
SUMMARY: An anthology of 50 poems about the seasons.
1. Seasons—Juvenile poetry. 2. Children's poetry,
American. [1. Seasons—Poetry. 2. American
poetry] I. Hopkins, Lee Bennett. II. Hague, Michael.
PS595.S42M65   811'.008'033   80-7983
ISBN 0-15-255291-X

First edition
BCDE

Contents

2122237

Autumn

September　MYRA COHN LIVINGSTON

Fall is coming.
I can smell it.
All the grass is dusty.

Fall is coming.
I can tell it.
Geraniums are rusty.

There Came a Day   TED HUGHES

There came a day that caught the summer
Wrung its neck
Plucked it
And ate it.

Now what shall I do with the trees?
The day said, the day said.
Strip them bare, strip them bare.
Let's see what is really there.

And what shall I do with the sun?
The day said, the day said.
Roll him away till he's cold and small.
He'll come back rested if he comes back at all.

And what shall I do with the birds?
The day said, the day said.
The birds I've frightened, let them flit,
I'll hang out the pork for the brave tomtit.

And what shall I do with the seed?
The day said, the day said.
Bury it deep, see what it's worth.
See if it can stand the earth.

What shall I do with the people?
The day said, the day said.
Stuff them with apple and blackberry pie—
They'll love me then till the day they die.

There came this day and he was autumn.
His mouth was wide
And red as a sunset.
His tail was an icicle.

Squirrel LILIAN MOORE

The squirrel in the hickory tree's a
nervous fellow,
all quiver and scurry.
See him

hurl himself upon
a limb
worry a nut
pack his cheeks
race
downtree
to a secret place and
hurry
back
in furry frenzy.

There's something he knows
that makes him
go,
this soft slow
mellow
autumn day.

It has to do with
hunger
in the snow.

Homework   RUSSELL HOBAN

Homework sits on top of Sunday, squashing Sunday flat.
Homework has the smell of Monday, homework's very fat.
Heavy books and piles of paper, answers I don't know.
Sunday evening's almost finished, now I'm going to go
Do my homework in the kitchen. Maybe just a snack,
Then I'll sit right down and start as soon as I run back
For some chocolate sandwich cookies. Then I'll really do
All that homework in a minute. First I'll see what new
Show they've got on television in the living room.
Everybody's laughing there, but misery and gloom
And a full refrigerator are where I am at.
I'll just have another sandwich. Homework's very fat.

Fall Wind   MARGARET HILLERT

I scarcely felt a breath of air;
I didn't hear a sound,
But one small leaf came spiralling
In circles to the ground.

And then the wind began to rise.
I felt it on my face.
It blew my jacket out behind
And made the white clouds race.

It seized the branches of the trees
And shook with might and main.
The leaves poured down upon the earth
Like drops of colored rain.

Crabapples   CARL SANDBURG

Sweeten these bitter wild crabapples, Illinois
October sun. The roots here came from the
wilderness, came before man came here. They
are bitter as the wild is bitter.

Give these crabapples your softening gold,
October sun, go through to the white wet
seeds inside and soften them black. Make
these bitter apples sweet. They want you, sun.

The drop and the fall, the drop and the fall,
the apples leaving the branches for the black
earth under, they know you from last year,
the year before last year, October sun.

Something Told the Wild Geese RACHEL FIELD

Something told the wild geese
   It was time to go.
Though the fields lay golden
   Something whispered, "Snow."
Leaves were green and stirring,
   Berries, luster-glossed,
But beneath warm feathers
   Something cautioned, "Frost."
All the sagging orchards
   Steamed with amber spice,
But each wild breast stiffened
   At remembered ice.
Something told the wild geese
   It was time to fly—
Summer sun was on their wings,
   Winter in their cry.

The Last Word of a Bluebird

As told to a child   ROBERT FROST

As I went out a Crow
In a low voice said, "Oh,
I was looking for you.
How do you do?
I just came to tell you
To tell Lesley (will you?)
That her little Bluebird
Wanted me to bring word
That the north wind last night
That made the stars bright
And made ice on the trough
Almost made him cough
His tail feathers off.
He just had to fly!
But he sent her Good-by,
And said to be good,
And wear her red hood,
And look for skunk tracks
In the snow with an ax—
And do everything!
And perhaps in the spring
He would come back and sing."

Pumpkins DAVID McCORD

October sun for miles and miles and miles;
and we were passing piles and piles and piles
of pumpkins—pumpkin-like, so like each other
no pumpkin knew one pumpkin from his brother.
If they were carved and placed in aisles and aisles,
with piles and piles of smiles and smiles and smiles
for miles and miles and miles on some dark night,
and one could handle, candle them, and light
the whole creation with Jack Pumpkinheads,
they'd be no wiser. What a pumpkin dreads
is being so conspicuous with eyes
and nose and mouth. Much better off in pies,
say pumpkins. So for miles and miles and miles,
with piles of pumpkins—aisles and aisles of piles—
just putting all their pumpkinheads together,
you couldn't tell what they were thinking: whether
they thought of Halloween, or where they grew
in yellow pumpkin fields. I'd say the view
was pleasing to those pumpkins at the top—
which were of course the best ones in the crop.
But since they had no eyes nowise to know,
they might as well have been down there below;
nor could they guess that mile on mile on mile
some boy was hoping he might see one smile.

Hallowe'en HARRY BEHN

Tonight is the night
When dead leaves fly
Like witches on switches
Across the sky,
When elf and sprite
Flit through the night
On a moony sheen.

Tonight is the night
When leaves make a sound
Like a gnome in his home
Under the ground,
When spooks and trolls
Creep out of holes
Mossy and green.

Tonight is the night
When pumpkins stare
Through sheaves and leaves
Everywhere,
When ghoul and ghost
And goblin host
Dance round their queen.
It's Hallowe'en!

Thanksgiving ANONYMOUS

The year has turned its circle,
The seasons come and go.
The harvest all is gathered in
And chilly north winds blow.

Orchards have shared their treasures,
The fields, their yellow grain,
So open wide the doorway—
Thanksgiving comes again!

Winter NIKKI GIOVANNI

Frogs burrow the mud
snails bury themselves
and I air my quilts
preparing for the cold

Dogs grow more hair
mothers make oatmeal
and little boys and girls
take Father John's Medicine

Bears store fat
chipmunks gather nuts
and I collect books
For the coming winter

Suddenly AILEEN FISHER

Suddenly the shops are bright,
changed by magic overnight—
red and green against the white.

Suddenly the streets are gay
as the carols begin to play
up and down, across the way.

And the children, young and old,
ruddy with December cold,
suddenly are good as gold.

Winter

Winter Dark LILIAN MOORE

Winter dark comes early
mixing afternoon
and night.
Soon
there's a comma of a moon,

and each street light
along the
way
puts its period
to the end of day.

Now
a neon sign
punctuates the dark
with a bright
blinking
breathless
exclamation mark!

Snowflakes   DAVID McCORD

Sometime this winter if you go
To walk in the soft new-falling snow
When flakes are big and come down slow

To settle on your sleeve as bright
As stars that couldn't wait for night,
You won't know what you have in sight—

Another world—unless you bring
A magnifying glass. This thing
We call a snowflake is the king

Of crystals. Do you like surprise?
Examine him three times his size:
At first you won't believe your eyes.

Stars look alike, but flakes do not:
No two the same in all the lot
That you will get in any spot

You chance to be, for every one
Come spinning through the sky has none
But his own window-wings of sun:

Joints, points, and crosses. What could make
Such lacework with no crack or break?
In billion billions, no mistake?

Snow FELICE HOLMAN

Softly
whitely
down
the snow
mounds
and sifts
in dunes
in drifts
coldly
sowing
fields
of clover
covering
December
over.

Winter Is Tacked Down   SISTER NOEMI WEYGANT

Hurrah!

Hurray!

It snowed last night.

Today
   the green lawn
     is whiskered with white.

Look around—
   enough snow on the ground
     for a snowball.

Scoop it up in your hands,
   gloves or no.
Wad it,
   pack it tight,
     round,
     big.

Let go!

Smash!
Splash!

Winter is here!

You can't hold winter back,
   not possibly,
     once you have tacked a snowball
     to the trunk of a tree.

Skiing   ROSE BURGUNDER

Fast as foxes,
buzzy as bees,
down the slope
on our silver-tipped skis—

early in the morning
Roseanna and I
far from our house
on the hilltop fly.

A snowbird's yawning,
the sky's all pink,
somewhere in the valley
the lights still blink.

No one's awake
but us, and a bird.
The day's too beautiful
to speak a word.

The Corner Newsman KAYE STARBIRD

It's strange about the newsman,
The one named Joe Malloy.
Along with having little
To laugh at or enjoy,
Why doesn't he wear mittens?
Why is he known as "Boy"?

He must be over sixty,
Yet all day long he stands
Selling whatever papers
The passing crowd demands
And blowing in the winter
Upon his chilly hands.

Sometimes I hate the people
On foot or in a car
Who holler, "Boy, *The Herald!*"
Or "Boy, I want *The Star*,"
While I keep thinking
How cold his fingers are.

That's why with Christmas coming
And all the trees aglow,
I bought some furry mittens
And tied them with a bow
And went around this evening
And offered them to Joe.

"Why, thank you, little lady,"
He said and stroked the fur;
And, though I wasn't certain
Just what his feelings were,
I said to him, "You're welcome.
A merry Christmas, sir."

New Year's Eve MYRA COHN LIVINGSTON

We got a broom (like Father said)
And just before we went to bed

We opened up the cold back door
And swept the old year out before

We ran to let the New Year in
The front, and told him to begin

And blew our horns and gave a shout
To see the old year running out.

A Winter Song WILLIAM J. HARRIS

If I
were the
cold weather
and people
talked about me
the way they talk
about it,
I'd just
pack up
and leave town.

And Then   PRINCE REDCLOUD

I was reading
a poem
about snow

when
the sun
came out
and
melted it.

Valentine Feelings   LEE BENNETT HOPKINS

I feel flippy,
I feel fizzy,
I feel whoopy,
I feel whizzy.

I'm feeling wonderful.
I'm feeling just fine.
Because you just gave me
A valentine.

FROM # March EMILY DICKINSON

Dear March, come in!
How glad I am!
I looked for you before.
Put down your hat—
You must have walked—
How out of breath you are!
Dear March, how are you?
And the rest?
Did you leave Nature well?
Oh, March, come right upstairs with me,
I have so much to tell.

Spring

Surprises Are Happening   JEAN CONDER SOULE

Surprises are happening under the snow.
Down deep in the ground things are starting to grow.
Protected from cold winds and ice by the mud
Rootlets are forming, then stalks and a bud.

Yes, Spring's on the way with its wonderful show.
Surprises are happening under the snow!

Early Spring   PHILIP WHALEN

The dog writes on the window
        with his nose

March ELIZABETH COATSWORTH

A blue day,
a blue jay,
and a good beginning.
One crow,
melting snow—
spring's winning!

Spring PRINCE REDCLOUD

How pleasing—
not
to be
freezing.

Spring KARLA KUSKIN

I'm shouting
I'm singing
I'm swinging through trees
I'm winging skyhigh
With the buzzing black bees.
I'm the sun
I'm the moon
I'm the dew on the rose.
I'm a rabbit
Whose habit
Is twitching his nose.
I'm lively
I'm lovely
I'm kicking my heels.
I'm crying "Come dance"
To the fresh water eels.
I'm racing through meadows
Without any coat
I'm a gamboling lamb
I'm a light leaping goat
I'm a bud
I'm a bloom
I'm a dove on the wing.
I'm running on rooftops
And welcoming spring!

Oh Have You Heard SHEL SILVERSTEIN

Oh have you heard it's time for vaccinations?
I think someone put salt into your tea.
They're giving us eleven-month vacations.
And Florida has sunk into the sea.

Oh have you heard the President has measles?
The principal has just burned down the school.
Your hair is full of ants and purple weasels—
                    APRIL FOOL!

FROM Two Tramps in Mud Time ROBERT FROST

The sun was warm but the wind was chill.
You know how it is with an April day
When the sun is out and the wind is still,
You're one month on in the middle of May.
But if you so much as dare to speak,
A cloud comes over the sunlit arch,
A wind comes off a frozen peak,
And you're two months back in the middle of March.

April Rain Song LANGSTON HUGHES

Let the rain kiss you.
Let the rain beat upon your head with silver liquid drops.
Let the rain sing you a lullaby.

The rain makes still pools on the sidewalk.
The rain makes running pools in the gutter.
The rain plays a little sleep-song on our roof at night—

And I love the rain.

How It Happens MARGARET HILLERT

The wink of a pink and shining eye,
The swish of a mischievous tail,
The jerk of a perky nose held high,
The flight over hill and dale,
The rush through the hush of Easter Eve,
The pause of a paw, and then
The Easter basket beside the door
And Easter gladness again.

FROM The Spring Wind CHARLOTTE ZOLOTOW

The wind I love the best
comes gently after rain
smelling of spring and growing things
brushing the world with feathery wings
while everything glistens, and everything sings
in the spring wind
after the rain.

Fueled   MARCIE HANS

Fueled
by a million
man-made
wings of fire—
the rocket tore a tunnel
through the sky—
and everybody cheered.
Fueled
only by a thought from God—
the seedling
urged its way
through thicknesses of black—
and as it pierced
the heavy ceiling of the soil—
and launched itself
up into outer space—
no
one
even
clapped.

Come soon.

Everything is lusting
for light,
thrusting
up
up
splitting the earth,
opening flaring fading,
seed
into shoot
bud
into flower,
nothing
beyond its hour.

Letter to a Friend

LILIAN MOORE

Come soon.

The apple bloom has melted
like
spring snow.

The lilac
changed the air,
surprising
every breath.

Now
low in the field
wild strawberries
fatten.

Come soon.

It's a matter of
life.
And death.

Analysis of Baseball   MAY SWENSON

It's about
the ball,
the bat,
and the mitt.
Ball hits
bat, or it
hits mitt.
Bat doesn't
hit ball, bat
meets it.
Ball bounces
off bat, flies
air, or thuds
ground (dud)
or it
fits mitt.

Bat waits
for ball
to mate.
Ball hates
to take bat's
bait. Ball
flirts, bat's
late, don't
keep the date.
Ball goes in
(thwack) to mitt,
and goes out
(thwack) back
to mitt.

Ball fits
mitt, but
not all
the time.
Sometimes
ball gets hit
(pow) when bat
meets it,
and sails
to a place
where mitt
has to quit
in disgrace.
That's about
the bases
loaded,
about 40,000
fans exploded.

It's about
the ball,
the bat,
the mitt,
the bases
and the fans.
It's done
on a diamond,
and for fun.
It's about
home, and it's
about run.

May   JOHN UPDIKE

Now children may
  Go out of doors,
Without their coats,
  To candy stores.

The apple branches
  And the pear
May float their blossoms
  Through the air,

And Daddy may
  Get out his hoe
To plant tomatoes
  In a row,

And, afterwards,
  May lazily
Look at some baseball
  On TV.

Summer

FROM **Stay, June, Stay!** CHRISTINA ROSSETTI

Stay, June, stay!—
If only we could stop the moon
And June!

To July ANONYMOUS

Here's to July,
Here's to July,
For the bird,
And the bee,
And the butterfly;
For the flowers
That blossom
For feasting the eye;
For skates, balls,
And jump ropes,
For swings that go high;
For rocketry
Fireworks that
Blaze in the sky,
Oh, here's to July.

The 5th of July FELICE HOLMAN

The moon moved over last night
    for bright sprays of fire
    big bursts of light.
    Fountains and candles
    and rockets zoomed by
    which seemed that they might
    burn some holes in the sky.

And the crowd cried "Aaah!"
    at the blinding displays
    of orbital pinwheels
    multiple rays
    that built to the final
    spectacular shower
    that made the plain night
    a sky-garden in flower.

Now, there's an arc of leftover light
    caught in the dark
    trapped by the night
    with pieces about it
    dotting the sky—
    a remembrance
    of the 4th of July.

The Errand   HARRY BEHN

I rode my pony one summer day
Out to a farm far away
Where not one of the boys I knew
Had ever wandered before to play,

Up to a tank on top of a hill
That drips into a trough a spill
That when my pony drinks it dry
Its trickling takes all day to fill;

On to a windmill a little below
That brings up rusty water slow,
Squeaking and pumping only when
A lazy breeze decides to blow;

Then past a graveyard overgrown
With gourds and grass, where every stone
Leans crookedly against the sun,
Where I had never gone alone.

Down a valley I could see
Far away, one house and one tree
And a flat green pasture out to the sky,
Just as I knew the farm would be!

I was taking a book my father sent
Back to the friendly farmer who lent
It to him, but who wasn't there;
I left it inside, and away I went!

Nothing happened. The sun set,
The moon came slowly up, and yet
When I was home at last, I knew
I'd been on an errand I'd never forget.

maggie and milly and molly and may
E. E. CUMMINGS

maggie and milly and molly and may
went down to the beach(to play one day)

and maggie discovered a shell that sang
so sweetly she couldn't remember her troubles,and

milly befriended a stranded star
whose rays five languid fingers were;

and molly was chased by a horrible thing
which raced sideways while blowing bubbles:and

may came home with a smooth round stone
as small as a world and as large as alone.

For whatever we lose(like a you or a me)
it's always ourselves we find in the sea

August MYRA COHN LIVINGSTON

Mike says
we ought to have
a swimming party.

Fine, I answer,
but where will we
have this party?

Here, he says,
pointing to the fire hydrant.
Here, he says,
when we turn it on.

We'll have a party
and invite
Alex and
any guy who wants to swim

Stand-
ing
up.

No Matter   LEE BENNETT HOPKINS

No matter
how hot-burning
it is
outside

when

you peel a
long, fat cucumber

or

cut deep into
a fresh, ripe watermelon

you can
feel
coolness
come into your hands.

What Shall I Pack in the Box Marked "Summer"? BOBBI KATZ

A handful of wind that I caught with a kite
A firefly's flame in the dark of the night
The green grass of June that I tasted with toes
The flowers I knew from the tip of my nose
The clink of the ice cubes in pink lemonade
The fourth of July Independence parade!
The sizzle of hot dogs, the fizzle of coke
Some pickles and mustard and barbecue smoke
The print of my fist in the palm of my mitt,
As I watched for the batter to strike out or hit
The splash of the water, the top-to-toe cool
Of a stretch-and-kick trip through a blue swimming pool
The tangle of night songs that slipped through my screen
Of crickets and insects too small to be seen
The seed pods that formed on the flowers to say
That summer was packing her treasures away.

Indoors   ROSE BURGUNDER

The doors are closing;
summer's gone:
harbor and hazard,
sand and sail,
hammock and haystick,
barn and briar,
fences and fairgrounds,
treetop, trail.

Now in my alphabet
of hours
are notebooks, numbers,
nary a lawn.
A clock ticks slowly
in the room.
Time is beginning;
summer's gone.

Taste of Purple   LELAND B. JACOBS

Grapes hang purple
In their bunches,
Ready for
September lunches.
Gather them, no
Minutes wasting.
Purple is
Delicious tasting.

That Was Summer   MARCI RIDLON

Have you ever smelled summer?
Sure you have.
Remember that time
when you were tired of running
or doing nothing much
and you were hot
and you flopped right down on the ground?
Remember how the warm soil smelled
and the grass?
That was summer.

Remember the time
when the storm blew up quick
and you stood under a ledge
and watched the rain till it stopped
and when it stopped
you walked out again to the sidewalk,
the quiet sidewalk?
Remember how the pavement smelled—
all steamy warm and wet?
That was summer.

Remember the time
when you were trying to climb
higher in the tree
and you didn't know how
and your foot was hurting in the fork
but you were holding tight
to the branch?
Remember how the bark smelled then—
all dusty dry, but nice?
That was summer.

If you try very hard
can you remember that time
when you played outside all day
and you came home for dinner
and had to take a bath right away,
right away?
It took you a long time to pull
your shirt over your head.
Do you remember smelling the sunshine?
That was summer.

Autumn CHARLOTTE ZOLOTOW

Now the summer is grown old
the light long summer
                    is grown old.
Leaves change
and the garden is gold
with marigolds and zinnias
tangled and bold
blazing blazing
orange and gold.
                    The light long summer
                    is grown old.

Acknowledgments

Every effort has been made to trace the ownership of all copyrighted material and to secure the necessary permission to reprint these selections. In the event of any question arising as to the use of any material, the editor and publisher, while expressing regret for any inadvertent error, will be happy to make the necessary correction in future printings.

Thanks are due to the following for permission to reprint the copyrighted materials listed below:

ATHENEUM PUBLISHERS, INC., for "August" from *The Malibu and Other Poems* by Myra Cohn Livingston (A Margaret K. McElderry Book). Copyright © 1972 by Myra Cohn Livingston; for "New Year's Eve" from *O Sliver of Liver and Other Poems* by Myra Cohn Livingston (A Margaret K. McElderry Book). Copyright © 1979 by Myra Cohn Livingston; for "Squirrel" and "Letter to a Friend" from *Sam's Place* by Lilian Moore. Copyright © 1973 by Lilian Moore; and for "Winter Dark" from *I Thought I Heard the City* by Lilian Moore. Copyright © 1969 by Lilian Moore.

THOMAS Y. CROWELL, PUBLISHERS, for "Suddenly" from *Skip Around the Year* by Aileen Fisher, Copyright © 1967 by Aileen Fisher; and for "Autumn" and the second stanza from "The Spring Wind" from *River Winding: Poems by Charlotte Zolotow*. Text copyright © 1970 by Charlotte Zolotow.

CURTIS BROWN, LTD., for "No Matter" by Lee Bennett Hopkins. Copyright © 1973, 1974 by Lee Bennett Hopkins; and for "Valentine Feelings" by Lee Bennett Hopkins. Copyright © 1975 by Lee Bennett Hopkins.

FOUR WINDS PRESS, a division of SCHOLASTIC MAGAZINES, INC., for "The Corner Newsman" from *The Covered Bridge House and Other Poems* by Kaye Starbird, text copyright © 1979 by Kaye Starbird Jennison.

HARCOURT BRACE JOVANOVICH, INC., for "The Errand" from *The Golden Hive* by Harry Behn, copyright © 1966 by Harry Behn; for "Hallowe'en" from *The Little Hill* by Harry Behn, copyright 1949 by Harry Behn, renewed 1977 by Alice L. Behn; for "maggie and milly and molly and may" by E. E. Cummings, © 1956 by E. E. Cummings. Reprinted from his volume *Complete Poems 1913–1962*; for "Fueled" from *Serve Me a Slice of Moon* by Marcie Hans, © 1965 by Marcie Hans; "September" from *The Moon and a Star* by Myra Cohn Livingston, © 1965 by Myra Cohn Livingston; and for "Crabapples" by Carl Sandburg from *Good Morning, America*, copyright 1928, 1956 by Carl Sandburg.

HARPER & ROW, PUBLISHERS, INC., for "Homework" from *Egg Thoughts and Other Frances Songs* by Russell Hoban. Text copyright © 1964, 1972 by Russell Hoban; for "Spring" from *In the Middle of the Trees* by Karla Kuskin. Copyright © 1958 by Karla Kuskin; and for "Oh Have You Heard" from *Where the Sidewalk Ends: The Poems and Drawings of Shel Silverstein*. Copyright © 1974 by Shel Silverstein.

Indexes

INDEX OF AUTHORS

INDEX OF TITLES

INDEX OF FIRST LINES